Times Change

Getting Dressed

Long Ago and Today

Lynnette R. Brent

Heinemann Library
Chicago, Illinois

Design by Herman Adler Design
Editorial Development by
Morrison BookWorks, LLC
Photo research by Carol Parden,
Image Resources
Printed and bound in the United States by
Lake Book Manufacturing, Inc.

07 06 05 04 03
10 9 8 7 6 5 4 3 2 1

**Library of Congress Cataloging-in-
Publication Data**
Brent, Lynnette R. 1965-
Getting dressed : long ago and today /
Lynnette R. Brent.
    p. cm. -- (Times change)
Summary: An introduction to how clothes and
the materials they are made from have changed
in the past one hundred years, discussing
clothing for all ages and all types of occasions.
Includes bibliographical references and index.
    ISBN 1-4034-4534-6 (lib. bdg.) --
ISBN 1-4034-4540-0 (pbk.)
    1. Costume--History--Juvenile literature.
[1. Costume--History.] I. Title. II. Series.
GT518.B74 2003
391'.09--dc21
                                    2003011103

Acknowledgments
The author and publishers are grateful to
the following for permission to reproduce
copyright material: pp. 1, 6(t), 14, 20, 24 Brown
Brothers; pp. 15, 21, 29 Photodisc; pp. 1(b-l),
14(b-r), 30(b-r) Diesel Footwear; p. 4 Image
Club; p. 5 Retrofile.com; pp. 6(b-r), 30(b-l) Levi
Strauss, Inc.; p. 7 Jack Hollingsworth/Corbis;
pp. 8, 26 Bettmann/Corbis; p. 9 Ariel Skelley/
Corbis; p. 10 Camerique/Retrofile.com; p. 11
Spencer Grant/PhotoEdit; pp. 12, 13 Corbis;
pp. 16(t), 22, 28 Culver Pictures; pp. 15, 21, 29
Photodisc; p. 16(b-r) Patrick Giardino/Corbis;
p. 17 Paul Barton/Corbis; p. 18 Minnesota
Historical Society/Corbis; p. 19 Patrick Ward/
Corbis; p. 23 Tony Freeman/PhotoEdit; p. 25
Michelle D. Bidwell/PhotoEdit; p. 27 Diaphor
Agency/Index Stock Imagery

Cover photographs reproduced with permission
of (t-l) Brown Brothers, (b) Photodisc

Every effort has been made to contact
copyright holders of any material reproduced
in this book. Any omissions will be rectified
in subsequent printings if notice is given to
the publisher.

Some words are shown in bold, **like this.**
You can find out what they mean by looking
in the glossary.

Contents

Long Ago

Imagine that it is long ago. It is late afternoon and you are playing sandlot baseball with your friends. You are wearing a cotton shirt, **trousers**, and suspenders. This is the only outfit you have to wear during the week.

As you slide into home plate you hear a loud rip. Your parents are going to be angry that you tore your clothes! Your only other outfit is for Sundays.

This is how you may have dressed if you were a boy living in the United States about 100 years ago. Let's see what other clothing was like in the United States long ago.

Boys often owned only one or two outfits. They wore the same outfit for school, chores, and playtime.

Clothes for Boys

Long ago, boys dressed as if they were small men. They wore **trousers** and blazers. Boys had only two outfits. They wore one of them during the week. The other outfit was for special occasions.

Boys wore the same kinds of clothes their fathers wore.

What Changed in the 1940s?

In 1873, Levi Strauss began sewing pants out of dark blue denim. They quickly became popular across the country with gold miners, cowboys, farmers, and other hardworking men. By the 1940s, children were wearing Levi's jeans as play clothes.

Long ago, denim jeans were only advertised as work clothes in catalogs.

Boys today often wear jeans for school and for play.

Today, boys do not usually dress like men unless it is for a special occasion. Boys have many more choices for clothes. Jeans are very common now.

Clothes for Girls

Long ago, many girls wore plain dresses with large collars, or yokes. They wore these clothes to school and at home. If a girl had only one dress, she could cover it with a clean pinafore, or apron, for special occasions.

Girls' clothes were often dark and plain because those fabrics were the least expensive to buy. Some of their clothes were bought from stores, but many were homemade.

Most girls wore the same type of plain dresses to school.

Girls today can wear what they like best.

Today, girls have many more choices in clothing. Girls still wear dresses and may even wear them to school. They also wear pants, jeans, overalls, and shorts.

There are many colors and types of fabrics to choose from. While some clothing is homemade, most items come from stores.

Clothes for Men

Long ago, men who worked in the city wore suits to their jobs. They also wore suits when they were not at work. A suit included pants, a jacket, a vest, and a tie. Men often dressed in formal clothes, even on the weekends.

Long ago, men wore suits even while spending time with their families.

Today, some men still wear suits to work, but most men do not wear them all the time. There are many different choices in men's clothes. Men can wear shirts, sweaters, turtlenecks, and many different types of pants. They wear these less formal clothes at work or on the weekends.

Men's clothes today are more casual and comfortable.

Clothes for Women

Long ago, many dresses had high collars and long sleeves.

Long ago, most women did not work outside the home. They wore skirts and blouses at home. Very few women wore pants. Those women who did work outside the home usually wore a long skirt with a blouse and a hat.

Today, there are many different choices of clothing for women. Some women still wear skirts and blouses to work, and their skirts can be different lengths. Women often wear jeans or other pants. At home, women wear more casual clothing like sweaters or T-shirts.

Today, some women wear suits to work.

Shoes

Long ago, shoes for men, women, boys, and girls were mostly high shoes that either buttoned or laced near their calves. The shoes had to be sturdy because with few sidewalks or paved streets, people had to do a lot of walking in dust and mud. People may have owned only one or two pairs of shoes because they were very expensive.

Women's high shoes were made to last a long time.

FASHIONABLE FOOTWEAR FOR LADIES.

THE EMPRESS.

No. 15H142

$3.00

PER PAIR

DON'T FAIL TO STATE SIZE.

A most natty button boot is this new style patent Eclipse coltskin beauty, made with glove calf top and the latest diamond tip. A thoroughly hand sewed shoe and an exclusive pattern of best quality. Sizes and half sizes, 2½ to 7. Widths, C, D and E. Weight averages 28 ounces.

THE COUNTESS.

DIAMOND QUEEN.

No. 15H144

$3.50

PER PAIR

DON'T FAIL TO STATE SIZE.

An advanced style, never before seen for less than $7.00. It is the latest craze in fashionable footwear. Made of best patent Eclipse coltskin and the new high wave top of dull mat calf. Has diamond tip, handsomely perforated throughout, short vamp and is bench made. Fitted with the latest "Hygienic"

THE PRINCESS.

No. 15H146

$3.00

PER PAIR

DON'T FAIL TO STATE SIZE.

A new Blucher style in a bench made button boot. Made of best patent Eclipse coltskin, with glove calf top, latest style heel and extra quality outer sole. Buttonholes are silk stitched and it is certainly a dressy shoe. Sizes and half sizes, 2½ to 7. Widths, C, D and E. Weight averages 27 ounces.

QUEEN OF BEAUTY.

Times Change

What Changed in 1955?

In 1955, Velcro was invented. This eventually became another way to fasten shoes and other pieces of clothing.

People have many kinds of shoes to go with different types of clothing.

Today, people have many choices for shoes. There are shoes with laces, buttons, Velcro, zippers, and some that do not fasten at all.

People own many different types of shoes for different activities. Different shoes are worn for dressing up, working, and playing. There are even different shoes for different sports.

Pajamas

Long ago, people wore long nightshirts and **nightcaps.** Pajamas were made from cotton or flannel. Since houses were cold at night, people needed to wear pajamas to stay warm.

The entire family often wore long, warm pajamas at night.

Times Change

What Changed in 1945?

In 1945, more and more houses were using oil burning furnaces. These furnaces kept houses warm all night. People didn't have to wear long, warm pajamas to bed.

Today, there are many choices for pajamas. People can wear nightshirts or nightgowns. Pajamas might have pants or shorts. They may be made from bright colors with different kinds of fabrics, such as flannel, cotton, and silk.

Today, pajamas come in a variety of colors and styles.

Dressing for Special Occasions

Long ago, families who could afford it had some fancy clothes. These were mainly for important days or for going to places of worship. Often, however, clothes for special occasions were not very different from everyday clothing.

Many women wore a new dress for their wedding. The same dress would also be worn to church on Sundays or for special occasions.

*Today, people wear fancy formal wear for special occasions, such as a **quinceañera**.*

Today, people wear fancy clothes for special occasions. If families go to worship, they often wear suits or dresses. Families also wear dressy clothes to events like weddings and funerals. This kind of clothing is sometimes called formal wear. It costs more than everyday clothing.

Hats and Gloves

Long ago, men often wore caps or **bowler hats** with their suits. Women wore large hats covered with items like bird feathers, velvet, and ribbons. People wore hats any time they were outside the home. Hats were an important part of fashion. Both men and women wore gloves.

Both men and women wore hats and gloves mostly for fashion.

Today, hats and gloves are worn for warmth and fashion.

Today, hats and gloves are still popular, but people may not wear them every day. There are many choices of hats today including caps, cowboy hats, and stocking caps. People usually wear gloves to keep their hands warm. Sometimes women wear gloves for formal occasions.

Dressing for the Weather

These girls were dressed warmly for ice-skating outdoors.

Long ago, people protected their shoes from rain and snow with **galoshes.** They also used animal fur in their clothing to stay warm. It was the warmest material at that time.

Today, people wear boots made especially for rain and snow. People also wear raincoats or **ponchos** to stay dry. New materials such as plastic have replaced most animal fur used in protective clothing.

Parkas help keep people warm today. Goose down is used quite often for winter coats.

Today, special clothing is available
to protect from rain and snow.

Sportswear

Long ago, people were just starting to become interested in free time. They were beginning to get involved in sports and other activities. Many new kinds of clothes were designed so people could roller-skate, bike, and play tennis.

Women started to wear skirts that were divided like pants for biking. People also liked swimming. However, their bathing suits covered most of their bodies.

Divided skirts made it easier for women to ride bikes.

Biking clothes today are designed for comfort and safety.

Today, there are even more types of different sportswear available. There are special clothes for soccer, gymnastics, track and field, and even biking. Bathing suits no longer cover most of the body. Both men and women enjoy sports outfits that are designed to be comfortable.

Making Clothes

Long ago, many women sewed clothes for the women and children of the family. Sewing machines were used if available. Women would also knit or **crochet** the clothes.

Men usually bought their clothes from stores or catalogs. **Tailors** made these clothes by hand. Sometimes they were made in factories.

It took women a long time to sew just a few pieces of clothing.

Times Change

What Changed in the 1900s?

In the 1900s, factories began to mass-produce clothing. This made garments cheaper and more readily available. People were able to go to stores and buy a wider variety of clothes.

Today, many pieces of clothing can be made quickly in factories.

Today, some people still enjoy sewing and making clothes for the family. However, the majority of clothing is made in large factories. These factories use heavy-duty sewing machines.

Caring for Clothes

Clothes were scrubbed on washing boards and then hung on clotheslines outside to dry.

Long ago, purchased clothes were expensive and handmade clothes took time. People had to be careful with their clothes. Washing clothes by hand and hanging them out to dry took a lot of effort.

Many people used pieces of iron that had to be heated on the stove before using them to press their clothes. Mending was done mostly by hand. **Cobblers** were available to fix shoes, although many people did this at home, too.

Times Change

What Changed in the 1930s?

Polyester was developed in the 1930s. This fabric and other new ones like it were easier to care for. They also lasted longer.

Today, cleaning clothes is more convenient. Many homes have washers and dryers, or people can go to a laundromat to wash their clothes. Dry cleaners are common. These are places where people can take their clothes to be washed or dry-cleaned, and ironed.

Many fabrics do not wrinkle, so people do not need to iron them. People are not as concerned about mending or repairing clothes and shoes since they are cheaper and easier to get.

Clothes washers and dryers make caring for clothes much easier today.

Clothing has changed a lot since long ago! If you open your closet, you might have more than one pair of shoes, and different clothes for playtime and special occasions. You probably even have lots of different kinds of socks, pajamas, and coats. New fabrics and new ways of making and caring for clothes help people have more choices when they get dressed.

Times Change

1873	1900–1910	1930–1940	1945	1955
Levi Strauss begins making pants out of dark blue denim.	Mass-produced clothing in factories becomes very popular.	New fabrics such as polyester and nylon are invented.	Oil burning furnaces are used to keep houses warmer all night long.	Velcro is invented. It later becomes another way to fasten clothes and shoes.

blue jeans

Velcro shoe

Glossary

bowler hat stiff hat with a round top and short brim

cobbler mender or maker of shoes

crochet needlework, like knitting

galoshes high overshoe worn in wet weather

nightcap soft, fitted hat worn with pajamas

parka very warm hooded jacket

poncho a piece of fabric worn as a jacket with a slit in the middle for the head

quinceañera a girl's 15th birthday celebration in some Latino cultures

tailor person whose job is making or fixing clothes

trousers pants

More Books to Read

Smith, Alistair. *Clothes and Fashions Then and Now.* Usborne Pub Ltd., distributed by Educational Development Corporation, Tulsa, OK, 1999.

Ask an older reader to help you read this book:

Hamilton, Sue & Hamilton, John. *Clothing: A Pictorial History of the Past One Thousand Years.* Abdo & Daughters. Edina, MN, 2000.

Index